LET'S GLOW GIRL

Learn to Rebuild Confidence From the Inside Out

Share your Story always!

Love & Glow,
Krissy Cressler

Krissy Cressler

Copyright © 2022 by Krissy Cressler

Publisher—Glow Up Media

Newburg, Pennsylvania

All rights reserved. This book is protected by the copyright laws of the United States of America. No portion of this book may be reproduced, stored in a retrieval system, or transmitted in any form or by any means, electronic, mechanical, photocopy, recording, scanning, or other. The use of short quotations or occasional page copying for personal or group study is permitted and encouraged. Permission for other usages must be obtained from eGenCo or the author.

Limit of Liability/Disclaimer of Warranty: While the author has used their best efforts in preparing this book, they make no representations or warranties with respect to the accuracy or completeness of the contents of this book and specifically disclaim any implied warranties of merchantability or fitness for a particular purpose. No warranty may be created or extended by sales representatives or written sales materials. The advice and strategies contained herein may not be suitable for your situation. You should consult with a professional where appropriate. The author shall not be liable for any loss of profit or any other commercial or personal damages, including but not limited to special, incidental, consequential, or other damages. The author is not suggesting or implying readers will duplicate these results. Most people who buy any "how to" information get little to no results, especially when they aren't willing to consistently follow the suggested strategies and work hard. All successful businesses incur risks and require persistence and action. If the reader is not willing to accept this, please do not purchase this book.

Library of Congress Cataloging-in-Publication Data
Library of Congress Control Number: 2022914175

ISBN: 979-8-9862024-0-2 Paperback
      979-8-9862024-1-9 eBook

Dedication

I am dedicating this book to my loving family: John, Max, Lennon, Spencer, Isaiah, Brylee, and Benton.

I am who I am today because of my oldest son Max, who has Down syndrome and has taught me so much about myself as a person and how to treat people. All six of my children have brought so much into my life, and I value all the life lessons I learn from them all. I am proud to be their momma! I hope I make all of them proud too, because my children's love means more to me than anything!

My husband, John, is my heart and soul, and I would not be where I am today in my life without him. He constantly believes in me and tells me how amazing and sexy I am, though at times I struggle to believe it. But without his constant encouragement, I would not be writing this book or be where I am in life. I am forever grateful for his love and support. I promise to always be there for you as you are for me. You are my forever and always!

How could I not thank my mom from the bottom of my heart for always being my biggest cheerleader! She tells me what I need to hear even if I hate it. I appreciate all her words of wisdom and support. She makes everything I need to do in my businesses possible by helping with all our children when John or other co-parents cannot. I hope to make her so proud in this life, and I can only hope to be half like her because she has the biggest heart of all.

There are so many people to whom I could dedicate this book that have impacted my life greatly. I am who I am because of all of you, and I'm so thankful to you all. I cannot name them all for fear of leaving someone out, but know if you have come into my life, then I dedicate this book to you, too. You, too, are a piece of my story.

Table of Contents

Introduction		vii
Chapter 1	A Small-Town Girl (With Big Dreams)	1
Chapter 2	Max – Overcome Fear	9
Chapter 3	Lennon – Never Give Up	17
Chapter 4	Spencer – Release Control	23
Chapter 5	John – Embrace Change	29
Chapter 6	Isaiah – Check Your Emotions at the Door	39
Chapter 7	Brylee – Stop, Listen, Grow	45
Chapter 8	Caroline – Sorrow Can Make You Stronger	49
Chapter 9	Benton – The Perfect Puzzle Piece	55
Chapter 10	It's Time to Glow Up	63
Chapter 11	I Am	73
About the Author		75

Introduction

When I decided to write this book, I was at a time in my life where every direction I turned took me to craziness. It was the beginning of 2020 and everyone's "normal" got flipped upside down. I have a beautiful, blended family with many situations, challenges, and a whole lot of fun, but raising six children is not an easy task by any means, especially in the midst of a pandemic. I run my own confidence workshop and spray-tan business at one brick-and-mortar location, and I also run a consulting and coaching business from home. I knew that my life was created for abundantly more, but every time I turned a corner, something would demand my time. I felt like I never had enough time for the things I longed to do.

With all this going on, I knew deep down that I had a message to share with other women and mommas out there, but it was a struggle to get it out there. All my time and energy was dedicated to being a great mother, wife, and businesswoman, and sharing my message always got put on the back burner. Writing a book had always been something that seemed possible, but when would I really take the time to actually do it?

One Monday, I was on a "Women of Power" call. That day, my husband had taken four of our children to the mountains for some outdoor activities and the house was still. A lady was talking about getting out of your own way and letting God lead you on the path He wanted to put you on. In that moment, I decided it was time to get out of my own way and let God lead me to tell my story. When the call ended, I sat down at my dining room table and the words poured out. With God's perfect timing and the encouragement of that call, I was able to dictate the rough draft of this book in the quietness of my home in a little less than five hours.

I wrote this book to tell you all about my challenges, successes, and chaos in life in the hopes that it will relate to somebody else struggling out there. I wrote this book to teach you how to glow up! Living inside your fears and your own limitations is not good, and it is not where God wants you. Believing that you were created for more and finding a way to fulfill that path is something many women struggle with. Now it's time to break through all those fears. It's time to stop limiting yourself with beliefs from the past and start creating the future that you deserve. You can create the life that God has intended for you and your family to live. There are no walls built around that life—only open space. The sky is the limit for you to feel free to live with joy in your heart. To wake up with a smile on your face and to go out there and be a beacon of light for other women looking for their answers. I call it the Glow Up!

Seasons of life come and go, and you can make any positive life changes you want, as long as you have the proper mindset. Is it easy? Absolutely not! Nothing in life is. I don't care what you do, there will always be challenges. The key is how you handle those challenges that will determine where you ultimately go.

Introduction

Your questions and answers are truly hidden within yourself. You just have to be willing to take the steps in the right direction to find them. I'm going to share with you some stories of my life—the joys, the sorrows, and the really raw parts. I will unpack some of my mindset beliefs and the things that have helped me get right with life where I am now, and what I need to do to propel myself in the right direction for my family's future.

To other mommas and women out there that are struggling through life, not knowing which direction is up or down, this book is for you. If you're looking to grow and change, to rebuild your confidence, this is your book. If you're looking to figure out how to work in the nooks and crannies of your day and also enjoy your family, this is your book. If you want to learn the art of self-care, how to enjoy some down time with a glass of wine, then this is your book. If you are looking to find and fulfill passions and just BE MORE, this is your book!

At the end of each chapter, you'll find little positive "I am" reminders. Put these reminders on sticky notes to post around your house. These will fill your head with bright thoughts and remind yourself of your goals. Sticky notes have saved my life—literally! I find I need to read and speak the positive "I am" statements daily to help me in the trying times of my days and keep my mind on a clear path. As we wear our many hats, it is important to have what we are still looking to achieve in front of us daily. The last chapter compiles all the reminders for you so if you don't have time to jot them down as you go through the book, you can write them all down at one time.

There is a chapter dedicated to each one of my children throughout the book, and there is a chapter about my husband. They have influenced my life and my business and are the main reason why I am where I am today. I have learned so much from each of them being a part of my journey, and the lessons they've taught me can help you through your journey, too. There are people in your life now that have most likely impacted you already, and you might not even realize it. The lessons those people teach you are going to help you find the very best you. So let's glow up together!

Chapter 1

A Small-Town Girl (with Big Dreams)

I was born and raised in a small town in Pennsylvania, and I now reside about eleven miles from there. I am an only child and never thought I would have children of my own. Yes, I said that. I never thought I'd have children. I was not a kid person. I wouldn't even babysit kids for extra money when I was growing up. But I was always an amazing student and I strived for straight A's. I worked very hard for those grades, and they did not come easily to me. I was a good kid, and I think my mom and dad would agree.

I spent my childhood in a trailer park. My parents were together for most of my childhood but divorced when I was fifteen, which caused some life changes in my teenage years. Those were some of the most impressionable years of my life. But looking back now, I wouldn't change any part of it. Instead of going to college, I got married young, and that marriage ended in divorce. Today, my first husband, Mike, co-parents our children with me. All of the hardships and positive experiences I had while growing up became life lessons and I've used them for good—for growth. But I didn't always feel that way. I believed a person like me would never be successful. How could I be successful and have a wonderful life if I was from a small town? This limiting belief I had kept me from getting to the next step of my journey.

Another limiting belief, one that many mommas face, came to me as I was raising my children. I was giving my all to them and helping them grow to become wonderful human beings in this world, so much so that I wasn't even thinking about my own goals and dreams. I believed there was no time for me to achieve those dreams of becoming a successful businesswoman when I was busy being a mom. How could I balance a life of excellent motherhood while owning a business? It was like I was surrounded by walls of defeat, and they were holding me back from reaching my potential.

I realized that I had many beliefs about myself that held me back from where I wanted to be in my life and my career and disrupted my positive mindset. My past experiences had created a large amount of limiting beliefs because of all the trials and tribulations I faced. When I started to understand the things that were holding me back, I thought more deeply about them and took time to understand and dismantle those limiting beliefs. This is when true success began to happen. I started to glow up.

Your mindset can make or break the direction your life takes you. Mindset is the key to everything! I have always been focused on learning and growing. I have set my mindset to understand that change is inevitable and is

Chapter 1: A Small-Town Girl (with Big Dreams)

a part of life. I use it all to stay positive and continue to grow.

In business or in life, you are on a journey of many ups and downs. You need to take the time to understand what holds you back in order to go further. This makes all the difference. Stopping and taking the needed moments to understand where you are in your journey and identifying where you need to grow is a struggle many people face. We're often so busy that we can't handle taking breaks of silence to think things through. We do many things for other people in our lives that we forget to listen to and take care of ourselves first.

I came to a point where I needed to stop and breathe. When I really paused and thought about what got me to where I am today, where I wanted to go in the future, and what was standing in my way of getting there, I was able to break through those limiting beliefs and make the changes I needed to be successful in my journey. I have no idea to this day how or when that mindset started, but at this point, I don't really care. All I care about is that I can see past that wall, and it doesn't exist anymore.

Since I took down those walls that limited me for so long, I have realized that I am a woman that can be successful and make a difference in the world. None of my past experiences define who I am today. I know God believes that I can, just as I believe I can, and that is all that matters! If you are living with limiting beliefs, you have got to eliminate them, and I want to help you. Believe that you, too, can do something great! Break the walls down, girl. It's glow time!

It's time to get your mindset right. You need to have faith—in God and in yourself. Get your faith in order and understand what it means to you. For me, my faith is first, then my family and friends, and then business. When I have those in balance, God always provides. You'll get to hear about all of that later.

It's important for people to wake up with joy in their heart and a smile on their face, to go into their day genuinely happy about what they're doing in life. If you cannot say that about your own life, then something needs to change! Why are you living unhappily? You have every decision at your own disposal—you are in charge of your life! You make the rules in this life. What life do you want to live? You get to decide how you wake up in the morning and how you view your day. So if you're not excited about what you do, maybe it's time to start looking deeper into what's going on in your life so you can make some changes.

Set a daily pace and plant seeds. You are living your life—maybe you're a momma or a career woman or both. You are busy and you are all over the place. You have to set a pace, set some standards, and tell yourself that you need to challenge yourself in order to feel good about the day. If you get a couple of important things done each day, then you will get where you need to be.

Sometimes it is important to embrace the chaos. People will tell you to find a work/life balance. But let's be honest, there is no such thing as balance when you have children, a household, and a job, or a business of your own. It is not always going to be perfect. When you're raising a family, things are going to happen. You need to learn to embrace the chaos of life.

I struggled to find that non-existent balance for many years. I thought I had to give a specific amount of time to one task, and then a specific amount of time to another. But it never worked that way and I'd be so stressed out at the end of the day. I'd beat myself up because I ran out of time. It's time to stop the nonsense and come to the realization that "balance" does not work. Instead of trying to find a balance of everything, I look at it as what I've heard as "creating harmony." Creating harmony amid chaos is what it is all about. When you figure out that harmony is what creates happiness in your life, you will wake up excited about what's in store for the day.

As you work on embracing the chaos, I also want you to focus a little bit on finding the calm in the day. When we embrace all the chaos, that doesn't mean we look at the world like everything's falling apart, even if it feels like it is. That just means it's time for a reset, to seek out the calm. It is a time to stop and think through what we need to do to grow on our journey.

When I finally found the calm, my business could flourish, and it ultimately led to a better relationship with my husband. Finding the calm is the part many women miss when they're building an empire with their business or raising children or maintaining their relationships with their spouses and friends. Many women go out into the world trying to help many other people and give so much of themselves that sometimes they forget how to really focus on what it is right for them and to find their individual greatness. The problem is, they are often so busy in life that they do not listen to the little signs telling them what needs to change. When they finally do make those changes, they give up on themselves too soon. You can find the greatness that is within you and speaks to your soul every day. When you least expect it, this greatness will tell you what you need to know so you can be aware of it and grab ahold of it. Every person has it inside of them to find. Whatever they choose to do with it is up to them.

To embrace your greatness, you must believe in yourself and to know that fear has no place in your life. You need to step outside of the fear and use your faith to guide you through obstacles and challenges that lie ahead. This will lead you on the road to your greatness, becoming the person God designed you to be. God has a plan for each and every one of us, and we need to take the time to understand His plan and live it.

Assessing your ideal traits and who you are, as well as recognizing where you need to grow, are key to becoming the person you want to be and finding out God's plan for you. When you decide to look deeper into these areas, you will discover a clearer path to becoming the best version of yourself. Once you determine who you want to become and a few traits you love about yourself, focus on your strengths to develop them even more. Then you will get a better picture of your dreams and goals—the full Glow-Up you!

We all have weaknesses, but focusing on them for too long will only make our journey longer. If we focus on those, we see how much we have to do to grow, and that can be so discouraging that we don't even want to try anymore. But right here at the beginning, focusing on all the attributes you like about yourself now will empower you to continue on your path to greatness. Then, when you have your dreams and goals in place, you will feel absolutely capable of achieving them. This is where your Glow Up journey begins!

Time to Glow Up!

It's time to assess who you are in the roles you play in your life. Choose three of your roles (for me, these would be wife, mother, and businesswoman), and then grade yourself in those roles. How well do you think you do in each of those roles? Write out your thoughts on a piece of paper.

Now ask yourself: How have your emotions and experiences allowed you to grade yourself in those roles? Write them down on the same paper.

Finally, consider your strengths in these roles. Where do you find yourself glowing already? Where do you think you could focus so you can improve in your roles? Write down all your strengths and write down one area to focus on in your growth.

Chapter 2

Max

Overcome Fear

New things in life can be scary. They bring all kinds of new thoughts, stress, anxiety, and fears that can hold you back from seeing the better side of a situation. I have had new situations come to me where I didn't know how I was going to handle them. All of the unknowns threatened to take over. How was I was going to move forward?

When I was pregnant with my first child, I was twenty-three years old and was overwhelmed with joy. Mike and I were so excited about having a baby and raising a child together. I was going to be bringing one of God's greatest gifts into this world. Many of my friends were having babies, and I was excited to experience the joy of pregnancy and motherhood they had. When it came to having a child, I thought that God was going to give me an easygoing pregnancy with a beautiful, healthy child, just like everyone else. I had painted this picture of what life would be like raising a baby. I never thought that I would be chosen to have a pregnancy filled with many unknowns and fears as we awaited the arrival of our precious child.

When we were told that our baby was going to be a boy, we also were told the alarming news that something was wrong with his heart. Of course, at the time the doctors didn't make a big deal out of it, guessing it was something that would probably heal on its own. They just told us that we needed some extra appointments to look further into it. And in my mind, I was okay with that, realizing that we probably would be just fine.

Through more appointments in the following weeks, the doctors told us some other things that were happening with Max. We were told his heart defect was one commonly found with Down syndrome children. It was an AV canal defect where he needed to have a wall put between the bottom two atria and a valve split for the blood flow. We were overwhelmed with a lot of doctor's appointments and many unknowns. He was safe and sound inside of me, but we would have a lot of things to deal with once he was born, such as surgery right away.

Mike and I decided to prepare. and we did a lot of research on Down syndrome and Max's heart defect. At the time we decided to not do an amniocentesis, which was the only way to figure out if he had Down syndrome. This was in 2004, and then it was a very risky procedure to do while I was pregnant. We didn't want the possibility of losing our baby. We were more concerned about his heart and what we would need to do once he was born. We knew that God had given us this child for a reason and to us, it didn't matter if he was going to have Down syndrome or not. All that mattered was that he was going to get treatment from some amazing doctors to ensure he would have a long life.

The weeks ahead and all the unknowns brought a lot of stress on me as I worried what the future would hold. When Max was finally born, he was diagnosed with Down syndrome, but all I could see was the most beautiful gift from God. I never thought in a million years I would be dealing with all these unknowns in life, but these unknowns helped me recognize that God's way is the only way and the perfect way.

Our struggles are given to us so we can see past ourselves and understand that we were created for bigger things. They strengthen us, sharpening us to be an example to others and to lift them up in their own struggles. These times are going to happen when you least expect it, but knowing that you can use your mindset to get past them in the proper way will guide you out of the bad times.

We each go through challenges in life, and we are faced with certain fears to see how we're going to handle them. I'm not going to tell you that I handled everything with grace. There was a lot of anxiety, fear, and things that we went through where I had moments of weakness. And that is okay.

It's important to remember that you're not alone. I was very blessed to have a strong husband who was my rock and to be surrounded by amazing friends and family through this difficult time. The prayers they sent us from the very beginning continued with us through Max's entry into the world. When you have a great circle of people around you to support and help you, you can get through those unknown situations more easily. Leaning on others can help you put some of those fears behind you. It shows you there is always light at the end of the tunnel.

Sharing your struggle with others works both ways, benefiting not just yourself but the people around you, too. Some people I've come in contact with let the fear paralyze them. They use those unknowns as excuses for not being where they want to be in life. If at any time you use your fears as an excuse to stay where you are, I challenge you to figure out why. What keeps you in those fears instead of letting yourself to continue on the journey to help other people? It is truly easier when you reach out and use those fears of the unknowns in those situations to help someone else. Share your experiences with others and assure them that they, too, will get through it and that they are not alone.

If more people were able to show others the way through these experiences, the world would be a better place. We all have to do our part, and sometimes that's really hard. Things are going to happen, and you will have no control over them. But it is how you handle those things that ultimately will take you to the place that you want to be, or at least get you on the right path.

Whatever your "Max" is in life, write your experiences down on paper and review them to see what you can learn from them. What knowledge are you gaining from this that may help you in a future challenge? The most important point here is when you take what you've been through in life, whether it's good or bad, you can use that to help others. That's all a part of glowing up. You never know who else out there has been through a similar situation. What if your story helps someone finally find a way to break down a wall? What if it helps them to remember and embrace that they're not alone, allowing them to see that they matter and that they can use those stories to become the best version of themselves?

You can use all the excuses under the sun as to why you aren't where you want to be in life. I know. I've done it before and sometimes I still do it. But if you sit down and look at why you allow that situation to hold you back and finally break free, you're going to see life in a whole new light. If you have a circle of people around you who support you and share your burden with you, it's easier to go through the rough times with them by your side.

Max is one of the most impactful things that has happened to me. He is now seventeen years old, and he is the biggest gift from God I have ever received. Max was the driving force behind me getting out of my comfort zone and trying to let my positivity rub off on other people when I talk to them. One of the things I love most about Max is how he loves others unconditionally, and he's taught me how to love people genuinely. Even though my life is still full of ups and downs and many challenges, the smile I see on Max's face every day is a message from God that I've got this. So I want you to figure out who your "Max" is. I want you to look at it every day and know that you've got this!

What would you say is God's perfect plan for you? Did it come out of something you never thought possible? I am living proof that it absolutely can. Stop and look back on your life and find the one thing that caused uncertainties in your life. Out of those unknowns and fears, eye-opening experiences can truly reveal God's perfect plan. If you haven't figured it out yet, it's okay. I promise it will come. The important part is that you become open-minded enough to see through the unknowns to the journey He has laid out for you.

Time to Glow Up!

Name a fear or an unknown situation that has happened in your past. What was the outcome of those unknowns? Was it positive or negative?

Write down what you learned from that situation. Even if the outcome was negative, know that that is okay. Dig deep and write down at least one positive thing that came from that situation, even if it's hard to find.

Think of something that is happening in your life right now where the outcome is unknown. What fears do you have? What positive thing can you focus on while going through this? Take the time to recognize those fears while also holding on to the positive.

Chapter 2: Max

STICKY NOTE MOMENT

I will embrace the unknowns and find a positive from every fear that comes my way.

Chapter 3

Lennon

Never Give Up

When I brought Lennon into this world at the age of twenty-six, I was super excited because I had prayed for another child. I was so blessed by what I learned about myself by having Max that I actually prayed for my second child to also be born with Down syndrome. While that might sound crazy to some of you, I loved who I became because of Max. I understood more about looking outward instead of inward. I learned so much by working my way through my fears that I became a truly real and heartfelt person. I was so engaged with what I was learning I thought maybe I'd be blessed even more with another child just like Max. However, God had completely different plans for me, and He knew exactly what I needed to help me learn even more about myself.

From the first moment Lennon was born, he was a firecracker. He was so full of energy, and he really knew how to cry, too! I never experienced a child like this before. If you know anything about Down syndrome children, you know that Max was the opposite of a normal baby. He never cried and he slept all the time. He had some health issues and was delayed in a lot of things. He didn't learn to crawl until he was one year old, and he didn't walk until he was two. So when Lennon was born, I didn't know what to expect. I knew it was going to be different, but I never knew just how much different.

One of the biggest things I learned from Lennon was how to overcome obstacles. No matter where you are in your life, obstacles are inevitable. But how you handle them and work through them will test your mettle and reveal what you're made of, equipping you to handle the next one in the future. Lennon was a child full of life, and he had a lot of struggles early on. He was lactose-intolerant, so I couldn't breastfeed him, and he would projectile-vomit until his lips turned blue. As a new momma to what I would call a normal child, I was in a completely different zone. I had no idea what I was doing, and I would sit there in a rocking chair holding Lennon while he screamed and cried. And I cried right along with him. I rocked him and talked to him, trying to console him as I prayed to understand what I could do to help him.

Through a lot of doctor's appointments and many sleepless nights, we finally started to figure out what Lennon needed to feel calm. We tried several formulas and fortunately we were able to find one that was just right for him. I will never forget the night when Mike and I finally found a formula that worked. When Lennon finished that first bottle, he had the biggest smile on his face. I remember looking at Mike and saying, "Wow, that is the most beautiful thing I've ever seen." My heart overflowed with

Chapter 3: Lennon

joy and happiness. After comforting Lennon, we finally found comfort ourselves.

When you come upon an obstacle in life, it is to teach and guide you into understanding another part of this amazing journey called life. How you view that obstacle and how you handle it is ultimately the most important part. Not every obstacle is going to be easily solved. It could take weeks, years, who knows how long, depending on the obstacle. How you progress past it will get you to the end lesson you are meant to learn.

Things aren't going to be easy, and you will go through a lot of trial and error. You may have to get out of your comfort zone long enough to open up to someone about the problem. You have to know where to turn and who to reach out to during this difficult time. But go into it with a proper mindset and ask yourself: How am I going to solve this problem? What is this problem going to need from me? Have I gotten through something like this before, and how did I do it? Do I need to look at this situation differently?

With Lennon, we had to dive in deep to figure out what was going on with him. If we had not, he may have had many months of discomfort, and we couldn't do that to him. We had to find a solution as fast as we could. For us, that required looking at things in a different way and changing our thought process. Even though I really wanted to breastfeed my son, my milk was only going to hurt him. I had to do what was best for him. It was because of our willingness to think ahead and be proactive that we were able make sure that from that moment, Lennon was a happy and healthy little boy.

All the obstacles that fall on your path are ways to grow. How are you handling yours? Are you wallowing in your misery? Or are you taking time to find ways around them? Are you thinking outside the box? Personally, I don't believe there is a box at all—I just don't create the box! Sometimes a shift in perspective is all it takes to get you through.

I am not a perfect person or mother. I still struggle with obstacles while raising Lennon. He is fifteen years old now and a full-grown teenager. For all of you moms out there raising teenagers, you know it poses a whole other avenue of problems. As those obstacles come up, my mindset is clear, allowing me to understand the problem and make my way through it in a positive direction. Because of that mindset, I can now move forward through my journey. As Lennon grows into an amazing young man, I see his ability to push through and bounce back when obstacles arise. He never gives up in anything he puts his mind to, and it's beautiful to see as he grows. He demonstrates to me every day that a never-give-up attitude is key!

I have heard it said before that other peoples' opinions do not pay my bills. This is so true! As you develop a never-give-up attitude, you also need to remember that people will always have something to say about what you are doing with your life. There is no way to stop people from judging or offering their opinions. But all you have to do is put their words in their proper place. Remembering that you are the captain of your ship and that you will never give up allows you to put all the noise behind you where it belongs. You keep being YOU and pursuing your visions. Don't let the naysayers make decisions for you. These are your dreams and goals to achieve, not theirs. Armed with a never-give-up attitude and the ability to overlook the opinions of others, you will continue on your path to achieve those goals and become your best you!

Time to Glow Up!

Think of a problem you are trying to solve right now. Grab a piece of paper and have your own vent session about the problem. Don't edit it. Don't think about grammar. Just write. When you're done, take a step back and ask yourself a few questions. Do you think you can solve it? If you don't, why can't you solve it? Have you put a box around the problem? How can the problem be solved? Are you still feeling hindered? Jot down your answers.

Go grab a highlighter. Now reread what you just wrote from beginning to end. Highlight any sentence where you talk down to yourself or any sentence where you make an excuse for why the problem can't be solved. Now flip the script. Take those highlighted negative thoughts and turn them into bright, positive thoughts. For example, maybe you said, "I am not smart enough to figure this out." Now say, "*I am* smart enough and *I will* figure this out." Problem solving is a learned skill. The more you do this exercise, the better you will get at it.

STICKY NOTE MOMENT

I can and I will find the good in every problem.

Chapter 4

Spencer

Release Control

I found out I was pregnant with Spencer when Lennon was six months old. I was absolutely shocked with the news. It was 2008, and Mike and I were looking at different health insurance options. In those days, when you were shopping for health insurance, a representative would come to your house to do the paperwork.

One of the questions the insurance agent asked me while we filled out the paperwork was when my last menstrual cycle was. "Why do you need that information?" I asked. He told me he just needed a date. I gave him a date and he did some calculations.

He looked up from his figuring and said, "The date doesn't really work out."

"What does that mean?" I asked. He said I should probably take a pregnancy test, because if we switched to this insurance and I was pregnant, the pregnancy would not be covered by the insurance. If you had a pre-existing condition, you would not be covered by the new policy, and pregnancy was considered a pre-existing condition at that time. Of course, I was shocked, but I agreed to do it. "But I'm pretty sure I'm not pregnant," I said. Even still, he wanted me to be on the safe side, so I agreed to take a test the next day.

I brought the test home and took it upstairs. Mike asked me what the verdict was. I hollered down the stairs, "I'm pregnant!" I knew the dear Lord had good plans for me, but I never would have guessed they included a third child while I had two other babies.

Life throws you curveballs, so you need to be ready for what you have no control over. They tell you to expect the unexpected, and let me tell you, the unexpected will come! Things in life are unpredictable and you absolutely cannot control everything. What you can control, though, is how you embrace these experiences, because they're happening to you for a reason.

It took me nearly two months to finally come out of denial that I was having another baby. Two-thirds of a trimester went by before I was ready to prepare for another newborn. It's really funny now because as Spencer is growing up—he is thirteen years old—he is the type of child that really likes to control things. I shared with him the story about how I found out I was pregnant with him, and it helped me explain to him that things will happen in his life that will be completely outside his control. Embracing these unplanned situations along your journey will guide you through other hard times in your life.

When life throws you a hard, fast one, it's normal to get upset, especially if it's something stressful or negative.

Chapter 4: Spencer

It's okay to scream or go off and cry over it. It is normal to react—believe me, I have those moments, too. But in the end, it's how you decide to handle it and how you project yourself out into the world makes all the difference. Projecting yourself into this world in a negative light is not going to better that situation. You can't glow up when you cloud your mind with darkness. It will only put more negativity out into the world, and you don't want that to come back to you. This is where I really want you to try not to overreact when something happens to you that you cannot control, especially in public.

I want you to experience what's happening to you by taking some time for yourself. Glowing up embraces self-care, which is super important. Taking time to process your emotions and just *be* is self-care. If you need to cry, then go ahead. If you need to scream, do that, too! If you are so stressed that you need to drink some wine, then indulge in a glass or two and take a moment to relax. Or you could go for a walk or draw a bath. But most of all, breathe!

Humans react first emotionally and then logically. It is important to step away from a situation and process it before responding. I want you to truly think over the situation that's happened to you and how can you handle it in the most positive manner possible. When it is done and over with, you can say you handled it with grace and professionalism, with heart, with kindness, and with everything that you know needs to be done. Your journey in life and what you're going through will help you understand what God wants you to learn, and it will also show people around you how to lean into the unexpected with grace and courage.

There are other people out there struggling through all kinds of things in life they cannot control, but I also know there are certain things they can control. Either they're choosing not to because they don't want to face the facts and learn from it, or their mind is so clouded by negativity that they simply can't see the way out. Once we turn the direction of our mindset to embrace the out-of-control things happening to us, your life will be more positive.

This will either take your life to another level or it will leave it where it is. Only you can choose the direction you want to take based on your mindset. Mindset in a positive direction is your key to success. Even if you have small amounts of positive thoughts, learn from them and try to look at things in a positive light. When you consistently take this outlook on new things and change your mindset, you will see more growth than ever before in yourself and in your life.

As Spencer grows up, I watch how he processes all the things around him. He is such a well-rounded kiddo, and he can see all sides of a situation. He has his moments like any teenager, but he mostly stays level-headed when complications arise. He teaches me every day how to keep my head up and look at everything from all sides. His whole life story has taught me to release control over the things I can't and to make good decisions over the things I can, and I am so thankful for that.

Chapter 4: Spencer

Time to Glow Up!

Write out the things you can control. For example, you can control your attitude on every situation, good and bad. You can control your vocal response. You can control your focus. You can choose to focus on negative aspects or you can choose to focus on positive aspects.

Remember that every choice you make affects your family, your children, your business, your marriage, yourself. You are in control. You can live on purpose. You can be the light. Even in situations where you feel like you are not in control, you still have control of how you respond in those moments. Choose the light. Choose to glow.

STICKY NOTE MOMENT
I am amazing at releasing control.

Chapter 5

John

Embrace Change

Change is inevitable and often uncomfortable. If you avoid it, though, you could potentially miss some of the most amazing opportunities in your life and some of the biggest blessings from God. I'm going to get vulnerable here again and tell you about something that helped me understand so much more about myself. I hope some of you can relate, but I also want to stress that I am not putting any one down or undervaluing what I went through. I look at all parts of my past as a positive thing. Every experience was vital for me to grow and get to exactly where God intended for me to be.

My first marriage was to my high school sweetheart, and we were together for many years. I was only fifteen when we met, and we were married seven years later. We bought a house and had kids, and believe me, those years were great. I learned so much about who I was from my marriage with Mike, and he was actually more like my best friend than my husband. Mike is an amazing father to all three of our sons. He is remarried now and has stepchildren, and a daughter with his wife.

Our divorce was better than many I've seen, and to this day I have a great relationship with my ex-husband. Many couples pull the children into the mix of ugly divorces. It's so hurtful to the children, and it breaks my heart. I didn't want that to happen with my kids. As our marriage ended, we made sure to protect our children and put their needs first. We focused on showing our children love and care as normal. It was very important to me to keep the peace for them. They were little and there was no room for Mike and me to show an unhealthy relationship when we were separated. I made it a point to keep the word "peace" all around me. I would buy every household picture or décor item that said "peace" on it. It was a way to help me always keep that in the center of my mind. We had challenging moments, which I'm sure happen in any divorce, but I worked very hard to keep my emotions in check, especially around the children. It was important they see all the good surrounding them, even if their parents were not living in the same house anymore.

One day, as I was driving back to town after dropping my boys off at daycare, I got a phone call that was very hard to handle. But I knew that I needed to process it. I pulled over into a parking lot so I could just sit there by myself and release all the things I was feeling. I remember crying nonstop and praying for about fifteen minutes. I had to get every bit of emotion out to put my head back in the game—to return to keeping the peace for my children. I remember a sense of peace came over me as I restarted

Chapter 5: John

my car and pulled away. God helped calm me so I could do what was needed that day at work.

As a mom, it can be hard to take time to process. Sometimes, we feel like we can't have those emotions anymore, but we absolutely can! When we process our emotions, we can get back to what we need to do, but we can also move on and feel refreshed by releasing what would normally hold us back from moving forward with our life. No one is perfect, but we all can choose how we process things and emotions in healthy ways without dragging others down in the process.

When I first met John, I was at a point in my life where I knew I needed change, but I wasn't sure if I could handle what was necessary at that time. At that point, I was still living in the world of limiting beliefs and convinced myself that since I had already been through a divorce, I was not going to be successful in finding love a second time around. I had been a single mother for three years before we met, and I would say those years were the most eye-opening of my existence. I was challenged with so many things, and I could have used excuses to stay stuck where I was during that time, but that would have held me back forever.

That being said, I did shut down for a few months and made excuses as to why I could never be the person I had always wanted to be. This was a time where I was trying to find myself. Trying to figure out who I was while raising my three children was difficult, and I started to lose myself. I was so wrapped up in trying to keep my marriage together, keep a household going, raise children, and try new things that over the years, I forgot who I really was.

I struggled with doing my favorite hobbies, like singing, learning to play my guitar, and going to concerts. My love for shoes and purses was immense, and painting was therapeutic for me. I always loved to read books that helped me learn and grow as a person. I loved gorging on romance novels and watching football and mindless reality shows when I needed down time. I lost my love for all these things along the way. It took about three years for me to figure out who I was again and who I wanted to become in the future.

There were experiences that happened during those years that I wouldn't wish upon anyone, but I do believe I had to go through those times to understand that I could choose which path of life I wanted to be on. Looking back now, I see God had His hands completely all over me and was guiding me right before I met John. God was showing His strength and light through me and giving me little hints and nudges of where I needed to be, what direction I should be going. If you are someone who married when you didn't know everything about yourself yet, then became a single mother and had to rediscover who you are while trying to find out who you can relate to, then you'll understand this. As I started figuring myself out again, I knew I wanted to find someone who understood me and my special needs child, who knew what it was like to divorce and co-parent while juggling your work schedule, your kids' schedules, and maintaining a household all by yourself.

Chapter 5: John

When John came into my life in May of 2014, I felt it was perfect timing. I was introduced to him through my family. John is my cousin Emily's husband's younger brother. Now, in a small town it seems like everybody knows everybody, but I never knew John existed until Emily mentioned him one evening. She and I were having a conversation about dating and moving on in life, and then out of the blue, she mentioned meeting Frank's younger brother, John. Up until this point, I thought Frank only had one brother. I was amazed. Remember, small town? I found out that John is seven years younger than I am, so we didn't go to school at the same time. He was in the Air Force and stationed in South Carolina, where he lived with his two children.

To that point after my divorce, none of the guys I dated had any children, which was strange to me because I thought I would only attract men that had children. But once again, God had bigger plans and knew exactly what He was doing. Change happens, and it can be so scary that some people would allow that change to paralyze them into staying complacent in their lives and not moving on. When I met John and his children and began to immerse myself in their lives, it was scary and new. I was going back and forth to South Carolina, and I was a rollercoaster of emotions, but there was something about him that made me feel like I was home. I hadn't had that feeling for years, and you are only given so many chances in this world to embrace what could be the biggest opportunity of your life. This can come in all shapes and forms. It can happen in relationships and in business opportunities. If you don't understand the necessity of change in your life, you could miss one of the most amazing things that could ever happen to you.

John is one of the most selfless, loyal, kind, dedicated, giving, trustworthy, hardworking, loving, and devoted men I know. He is exactly what God had planned for my life to give me a second chance at forever and really become who I was designed to be. He supports me in everything I do, no matter what it is, and he always has my back. He even brings me coffee in bed, and that definitely makes him a keeper! In the beginning of our relationship, it was like we had known each other forever. We hit it off quickly, and that is an understatement. We instantly had a connection and were able to talk on many different levels. Both of us had the same feeling that we were meant for one another. It was difficult for us to get time alone because we were in kid mode from the moment we met. We made the most of the time we had with just us. I always said it was important to me that we get to know each other as "just us" and not only "us with children."

John understands my passions and my desire to help other people. He knows when I'm down and being too hard on myself. When tough things come up and I start getting negative, he is the first one to tell me to knock it off and that everything is going to be okay. I look at him and tell him he is right. And guess what? He is (most of the time...wink wink). He is one of the most amazing things that has ever happened to me.

I feel he was perfectly timed and put in my life by God. My limiting belief that I did not deserve a second chance

Chapter 5: John

at love and happiness was ripped apart and thrown in the trash! Had I not opened my eyes to see the changes that were necessary in my life, I never would have met him, and I guarantee I would not be writing this book right now. I would not be surrounded by such amazing and loving people in my life, and I would not be as blessed as I am with all my wonderful children. I now have two incredible stepchildren and another beautiful son that we had together. As John and I grow in our relationship together, I feel fulfilled and appreciated. As life goes by and we continue to raise our children the best we can, we are growing as a partnership more and more. God's plans are perfect! I give all the glory to Him for allowing me another chance to have love and to follow my dreams. John was God's gift to me and the reason I am where I am today!

When you are presented with something in your life that offers you a huge change, you have two choices. 1) You can go all in on that change and embrace it—to look at it in a positive mindset of where this change could take you, and 2) you can turn your back on this change, stay complacent, and keep doing what you've been doing. Look at these as doors of opportunity. You can continue to move backwards in life and never be what you truly know you are deep down inside of your heart. Or you can walk through that door.

Through the door is probably something you have been praying for. You just need to be able to recognize when it comes to you. You need to be able to listen and know that when that door is in front of you, you grab it while it's open! Many people do not grab the door, and it shuts because they are too caught up in their own minds and the "what ifs?" They miss those opportunities because of worries and fear. I urge you to be open to listening, watching, learning, and growing, because opportunity will come sometimes when you least expect it.

You have the power to choose what you do with change. In your Glow Up, you get to decide where you want to be and release those limiting beliefs. It is your choice, and nobody can make it for you. You have to decide where you want to be, and you have no one to blame but yourself for what you do with this change. If you are faced with one of the biggest, life-changing things to decide, what are you going to do with it? How are you going to view it? Do you open the door and walk through it? Are you going to be able to achieve everything you've ever wanted in life and be the person you've always wanted to be with this change? Or is it a change that could destroy you and hold you back from everything you know could be. When you're faced with a big change, ask God for strength, view the change with a positive mindset, and keep grace in your heart. You have a willingness to push, and you will succeed through the change.

Your life requires a leap of faith from you. During the changes, make sure to always make time for yourself. What changes are you faced with right now in your life? How can you view them differently so you don't miss out on the amazing side of the change? What are some self-care things you have always wanted to do but keep putting off? Make sure you write one down and prioritize focusing on you and caring for yourself in the next week. Find a friend to do this with so you can hold each other accountable. Write up sticky notes to remind you of what you want to do and surround yourself with them so you can make it happen! Once you do, you will feel empowered to continue to do your best going through your seasons of life.

Time to Glow Up!

What is one change that you struggled with recently? How could you have handled it differently? Take out a pen and paper and jot down some thoughts. This exercise will teach you how to evaluate things happening in your life and how to find a new perspective on them.

Think of doors of opportunities you have been faced with. Did you walk through the door or did you stay in your comfort zone? Your comfort zone is blocking your way to the door of opportunity. Now write down some pros and cons of getting out of your comfort zone to open those doors. For example, you want to start a new business. Some cons are that you are going to need to get childcare. You won't be home to cook dinner every night. It could be a financial strain on the family while you're starting out. Some pros are that you will learn new skills. You can be your own boss. It could financially benefit your family more, allowing you to get more family time and go on more vacations. You may even be able to pay for your kids' college.

Look at your list, and focus on the pros. Are there enough pros to break down your comfort zone and step through that door of opportunity? There will always be scary parts of taking the leap, but if you stay focused on the pros, you will have the courage to walk through the door.

> **STICKY NOTE MOMENT**
> I will step out of my comfort zone to walk through my doors of opportunity.

Chapter 6

Isaiah

Check Your Emotions at the Door

It is time to check your emotions at the door and put them in their proper place. When I met John, he had two children, Isaiah and Brylee. They are both my stepchildren now, and I couldn't be more grateful. The first time I met Isaiah in South Carolina, I thought he was a ball of fire! He was so full of energy, bouncing here and there. I remember him literally standing on top of the counter, jumping down, and then running out the door. I was kind of shocked by it, because while my boys were full of energy too, this was a new type of energy with a lot of emotion behind it.

He was completely different from my other children. One minute Isaiah would be happy-go-lucky and the next he was screaming and crying and on the ground. I never experienced that with any of my boys up until this time, and I was taking it all in. I didn't have a lot to say at first, but I tried to guide him anyway. It was difficult, but I tried to find out where his emotions were coming from during these episodes. One of the biggest things I learned as he became a part of my life was how we handle his emotions and how we make sure they are dealt with properly. I started to use some of the knowledge, resources, and networks I gained from having Max and Lennon to help me figure out how to help Isaiah.

There are situations that happen as we grow older that spark emotional responses, and we have to put ourselves in the child's frame of mind, acting like a child does when they're first learning these emotions. What do we do with these emotions? What can the child get away with? How much energy gets put out there? What will a parent do? All of these things will happen, and we have to understand what emotions can do.

Emotions can either make things better or make them much worse. When you understand what you're feeling in all your different roles, how you handle them on the outside will make or break a situation. We all have emotions that we act on, and we all are going to make mistakes. Figuring out how to handle them in a positive way is key. When you are in an emotional situation, take note of it by working through it. Writing down what you're going through will help you to understand where your emotions are really coming from.

Your emotional reaction to your situation will make a difference in its outcome. When a business deal or a situation in life isn't going the way you planned, it doesn't mean that you take what you're feeling at that time and throw it out there, responding without processing it. Sometimes it's just not worth putting out into the world—not on your social media pages, not in a text. Voicing your emotions to someone too soon can cause a negative response. You need to handle those emotions with grace and thought. There are times in my life where I have not responded that way, but looking back, those situations helped me learn and grow.

Just take a few seconds the next time something happens to check those emotions at the door. When you check your emotions at the door, it allows you to be professional and consistent with your mindset so you can understand and control the emotions you want to present. It is important to understand emotions are necessary and that we all have them. We all have a right to speak to them or feel them, but make sure that how you want to be perceived by others is what you're putting out into the world. If you're bashing on other people's posts on social media or even if you're dealing with your children a bit too rashly, think about those situations and try to learn from them. Try to understand where those emotions come from and where they belong.

I especially urge you to also think about this when it comes not just to handling your business and the people around you, but how you handle your children. Putting good into your kiddos' minds is extremely important, but they also have to see you being that good, doing good deeds, and helping others. They must see it, not just hear it. Your children are going to do what you do, not what you say. Our children watch us every day and follow our lead much more than they listen to the words we say directly to them. You can tell them everything you want, but they have to see that you're handling your situations appropriately so they mimic that behavior someday.

Are we perfect? Absolutely not! Believe me, I do not have this down to a science. But I am learning through all of this just as much as you are. I'm just as much at fault for making mistakes and reacting emotionally. But as soon as I catch myself, I apologize for what I'm saying. I catch myself every week doing something that I'm telling my kids not to do and am hit with the realization that I need to show them, not tell them. When you realize this and are able to catch yourself, that's when you know you're on the right path. That is when you can truly make changes in your life to better yourself, your children, and to help them grow and develop into the people that you know that this world needs.

Let's make a pact together. Let's decide together that we are going to check our emotions throughout our daily lives and put them into perspective before we respond. This way we can show our children and lead by example in things that come at us unexpectedly. For example, let's say you are dropping off your children at school and one of them gets sick in the school parking lot (yes, this is one from my personal life). Your immediate reaction is *Today is NOT the day! I am extremely busy with meetings and appointments. You can't be sick now.* What do you do? Get frustrated that your day will be turned around? Yes, that can happen, and it's totally okay to be frustrated as you are processing what just happened. But if you can just look to the moment and breathe through it while you process and think, *How can I problem-solve the rest of this day? Can I do the meetings from Zoom? Can I reschedule the appointments? Is there someone to help later in the day so that I can push the schedule back? Or do I just scratch the day and stay home?* You get to choose the next step you take in your day. That is the best part of glowing up! This is a golden opportunity.

We humans are first emotional and then logical. This is a fact. The beauty of checking your emotions at the door is all about pausing, processing, and then speaking. We are also not perfect, and you will not always be able to do it well. But instead of reacting to a situation, find a way to look at it in a different viewpoint before going right into react mode. Process the information, think through your response, and then speak. Step out of the room if you need to. Give yourself the time to process. If you process the situation and use it to learn, then you are a huge step ahead for the next unforeseen situation.

Let's show our children how we handle these emotions in the best way possible so that we can show them how to do it the same way when they grow up. For all of you mommas out there who want to take the challenge, now's your time. Start today!

Time to Glow Up!

Think about a time when you reacted poorly to someone. I am sure you regret it. Or maybe you don't. But how could you have handled it differently? Write down some things you could have done in the example above that would have allowed you to not react the way you did.

> **STICKY NOTE MOMENT**
> I am in charge of my emotions.

Chapter 7

Brylee

Stop, Listen, Grow

Brylee was a tiny little girl with the sweetest curly locks. She pronounced my name with a "T" instead of a "K," and the way her sweet lips said "Twissy" brought a smile to my face. She was adorable and smiled so much, but she was very quiet and tended to keep to herself. We would all be talking to each other, and she would just look at us and smile without a word. I had a hard time communicating with her in the beginning, and it was really hard to break through. In those early days, I treated her quietness as a barrier because I thought she just was shy with me as a new person in her life.

As I got to know her better, I realized that it was just her nature. Though she was quiet, she took in all that was happening around her when she was young, and it made her become such a wonderful child. She might still be quiet to this day, but in her quiet, she has taught me so much. She is something I am not. Sometimes I would think she was more mature than most teenagers. But she was so young, how could that be? I'm an outgoing person who talks non-stop, so it was hard for me to understand her silence when I was beginning to know her. We were complete opposites when it came to how we communicated. But my mother reminded me that when I was a little girl, I was a very quiet and shy. Now, of course I don't remember those days, but learning that I was like Brylee as a child helped me to relate a little more with her and understand her more.

The quiet times and the silence are not always bad things. A lot of times when people are dealing with difficult situations, they react impulsively instead of taking the necessary time to stop, think, and understand what's going on. I understand in life it can be tough to work on everything that needs to be dealt with, like running a successful business or raising a happy family, plus taking the time to break through certain areas to continue to grow. It is so important to take moments to enjoy the silence.

Stopping and thinking has allowed me to break through and achieve my goal of finding success in my family, in my businesses, and in helping other people do the same. It is during these times of silence where you can think things through, and it leaves you more open to have an "ah-ha" moment, bringing you to a clearer understanding. God will talk to you when you are open and will allow you to burst through those limiting beliefs from your past.

Through having Brylee, I saw that silence is actually a gift to be cherished. Although my natural tendency is to go-go-go, it is vital to pause, be still, and reflect. This stillness allows you to self-evaluate so you can best take care of yourself. I believe that standing still in the silence can be self-care. These last few years have given me many challenges, and I am grateful for my moments of silence so I could process the path God wanted me to be on. Embrace the quiet moments because sometimes they are necessary for growth. I thank Brylee for teaching me this lesson and for reminding me how to just be, and from there God has it!

Time to Glow Up!

Take five minutes and allow yourself to sit in silence. Just stop. Lock yourself in the bathroom or your closet and just be with yourself. Set a timer if you need to. When the five minutes are finished, write down anything that came to your mind. Did you have any new ideas? Did you only think about things that are stressing you out? Did you think of answers to things that are stressing you out? Did you think about nothing at all? It is a gift to be able to sit, be still, and reflect on the quiet. Try to integrate finding that quiet into your life, even if it's only once a month.

STICKY NOTE MOMENT

I am able to stop, listen, and just... be.

Chapter 8

Caroline

Sorrow Can Make You Stronger

Shortly after John and I met, we found out we were expecting a baby. We did not plan on having a baby so quickly. We both understood that if it were God's plan for us to have a child together, so then so be it. We started to finally embrace the fact that we were going to be bringing a new baby into this world. To be honest, I did not anticipate having any more children. Many years had passed since I first had my children in my twenties. But if God had bigger plans in store, then that's exactly what we were going to do.

I was thirty-three at the time, and we started to really talk about our future and what it would look like to merge our lives together. Even though we had been together for a short time, I felt like I had always known John. We could talk so easily, and it seemed as though we had known each other forever. That's when I knew God had put him into my life at the right time. Despite being older, we were excited about having a baby. I think John was the most excited! Despite all this joy, I was a little nervous about the toll it would take on my body. Needless to say, we were ecstatic as we waited to bring this wonderful bundle into the world.

We weren't very far along in the pregnancy when I was in a minor car accident with my mom and my aunt. I went to the hospital, and they did an ultrasound on my unborn baby. They had a hard time finding the heartbeat. They set up a few other appointments for me in the next few weeks.

They discovered that the baby wasn't really growing like they had hoped. My hCG levels were not where they needed to be, and the following week we were told there was no heartbeat at that time. I wasn't able to naturally pass the baby and had to go in for surgery to help that process along. It was one of the most raw and emotional things I've ever gone through. After many weeks of preparing our minds and hearts for this new and exciting journey that was unfolding, this was completely unexpected. We had been so excited and now, in a moment, all of that had changed. We were shocked and overwhelmed by a sudden sorrow that changed the way we envisioned our future, leaving us with many unknowns. Though we would never meet her, we named our baby Caroline because she was created in South Carolina, which was something that was very special to us.

Going from so much joy to so much sorrow was hard to process. The rollercoaster of emotions I felt were a struggle. Even still, the feelings of joy followed by sorrow made me a stronger woman. I was able to remove myself from the whole situation and look at it from the outside.

It helped me to understand what was happening and why it had happened. I used it to grow into a more compassionate woman.

This experience made me realize how strong I was and gave me a deeper love for all of my children. It deepened my desire to have another child because I felt that I now had something missing in my life. I knew this happened to John and me for a reason, and it made us seriously discuss what direction we wanted our lives to go in. After talking more in-depth about it, we felt it would be meaningful to the both of us if we tried to have another child together.

When you go through the loss of a child, no matter before birth or once born, people handle things differently and look at them in a different way. Caroline was a part of our life for only a short time, but she will live on forever in our hearts. Life is precious. You only get one life, and you must embrace it and make the most out of it.

Use your life for the good when it comes to raising a family, taking care of a house, running a business, doing your job, being the best you that you can in everything you do in life. Look at your actions and how they are making you feel. Try to understand that sometimes you can't control everything that happens to you, but there is a reason behind it. It's up to you to use the joys and the sorrows to grow into a place where you can heal.

Healing is a vital, important part of life. Healing makes us stronger individuals and helps us to be better mothers, wives, business owners, employees, or whatever it may be. We also take that time to use the support of caring people around us that provide us with strength.

Things can happen quickly, and emotions can take over your life at the most unexpected times. It is at those times when you can develop the strength that you didn't know you had. You can push through and focus on what that joy and sorrow felt like. You can use that to help someone else in the future that may be going through a similar time in their life. Try to use your newfound compassion and understanding to be there for a person who needs it.

I want any other mommas out there that have gone through a similar situation as this to know that my heart goes out to you. You are amazing, you are strong, and you are worthy of peace and understanding. You are not alone, and there are people out there for you if you need to talk about your feelings, your pain, and your sorrow. Find someone to open up to and share with to help you find healing. If you've been through this struggle and have moved through your sorrow, maybe you could reach out to someone else that is struggling. You can find a support group and volunteer.

If I have learned one thing, it is that women showing support and comfort to other women goes a long way. Women supporting women should be important in our current culture. We all grow much stronger if we have one another to lean on. I am giving love to all of you mommas who have experienced a loss of an unborn child. There is a large group of women out there who can support you if you ever need it. You are not alone.

Chapter 8: Caroline

Time to Glow Up!

Call, send a text message, or write a card to someone that may be struggling through a situation. Take this moment to encourage them and bring some joy to them. If you need that healing or are in a place of sorrow yourself, I challenge you to reach out somebody — a friend, a family member, a support group — and find the support you need. Remember you are not alone.

> **STICKY NOTE MOMENT**
>
> I can walk through sorrow to find joy.

Chapter 9

Benton

The Perfect Puzzle Piece

Think of your life like a puzzle. Except there isn't a box with a pretty picture that shows you what it should look like when you put all the pieces together. The pieces come together as you progress in life, and the picture grows and changes as you evolve in your life. The outcome is unknown but it's up to you to design.

When I married John, my puzzle grew tremendously as our lives blended together. When Benton came into the world, we anticipated the exciting things that a new baby brings. We merged our lives together with both of our children, and now we finally had our child together. Benton is the perfect piece of our puzzle, and he completes our blended family. He is the most beautiful but not-so-little bundle of joy—entering the world weighing ten pounds and five ounces. Yes, I said that right! He was a big boy, so I ended up have a Caesarean section, and I praise God I had a one. That is all I'm going to say on that subject! Here was one of the biggest blessings from God—literally—and I was so excited to have him.

Let's Glow Girl

I was just a month shy of my thirty-fifth birthday when I had Benton. My pregnancy was hard, and for any of you mommas out there that have had babies in both your twenties and thirties, you know it's different in your thirties. My body was confused about what was going on and wasn't happy I was doing this again! Guess what? We did!

He is a little bit of John and a little bit of me. When he was first born, he looked just like John, and it was like I had no work in making this child at all. I was a little bummed, but I will say as he started growing and getting bigger, he is now a complete combination of all the good of John and me put together. I never thought that in a million years that our little six-year-old boy would have brought everything together in our family and make it feel complete. He truly is the perfect little puzzle piece. It's really funny, though, when you think of things going on in your life and the way you look at some of those things. You fixate on them, and sometimes you can get downright upset about them. You ask yourself, "Why is this happening to me?"

Things happen in life, and we often wonder *why*. Sometimes you don't know what you're missing in your life because you're so worried about everything that's going on and fixating on all the wrong things. You can't even understand what it is you're missing, and you sometimes will pass by amazing opportunities because you're so focused in the wrong direction. You will think in your mind that you've got to find this perfect man, relationship, perfect house, and perfect job. When you look at things in the wrong way, it's usually because you're not seeing it in the way that God has designed it for you. You may miss it because your focus is on all the wrong things.

You try to just put all these pieces together yourself, and in the end, when you look at the puzzle, you ask yourself, "What am I doing with my life?" Nothing feels right and it's all a mess. Your worry about the mess becomes so large that you can't even see what's in front of you. You're missing that perfect puzzle piece in your life, and all the answers you seek could be there.

When we lost Caroline, it exposed to us a desire that we didn't realize we had. Once we felt that desire, we decided to pursue it. We were so blessed to have Benton, and he has been the perfect puzzle piece to our family. You may be reading this and thinking of areas in your life where something is missing. Look at your life and try to understand where you want to be in the future. I encourage you to pursue that potential passion.

Chase down the people who have what you want, whether that's a thriving marriage, a successful business, or maybe someone who can teach you how to crochet. I don't know. What's your passion? Explore it. Pursue it. Your puzzle piece can just be around the corner. That puzzle piece can literally make a difference in your life. It may just be how you advance to the next step of your journey.

A lot of people will look in all the wrong areas. They go to the wrong people to ask for information about things that they know nothing about. If you're looking to find the perfect job, the last person you're going to speak with is someone who is miserable in their job. If you want to find the perfect business that fits your passion, you're not going to ask somebody who is unhappy with their business. I don't think you're going go to a friend who has had multiple bad relationships for advice on how to find the perfect man. Let's be honest, in none of these scenarios do these people have any idea of how to help you find your perfect puzzle piece.

Talk to people who are where you want to be when you are looking for your passion or trying to become a better person. It starts with who you surround yourself with and who can support you in your journey. There are many people out there who will try to give you advice in all aspects of your life with no knowledge of what you are searching for. If you take that advice, your puzzle piece is not going to fit. You may get frustrated because you are spending so much time trying to put the wrong piece into your puzzle. Look for people who are going to help you see things in a way to that helps you design a puzzle piece that will fit perfectly and fulfill your passion.

Being the best wife, mother, or business-owner is possible. Now, we all know we're not perfect, let's make that clear, not even the people you look up to. I want you to understand that you need to be searching for people that have what you want in life, that are going in the direction you desire to walk in. Reach out to them and say, "Hey, I see what you are doing, and I want that. Can you guide me and show me how to get there?" Find people who can help you grow in all areas of your life.

Maybe you want to grow in your time management skills. We have craziness in our house with multiple children and I'm not going to sugar-coat that part, but I manage to handle a special needs kiddo and all the things that entails, including doctors' appointments and schooling. I help all our kids with their school, sports, doctors, all while running a spray tan business and confidence workshop. I also run a consulting and coaching business from home, and volunteer in our community. I am sure there is so much more that I'm missing!

People ask me, "How do you take care of your household and business and make a daily plan of action to make things go more smoothly?" It all comes down to my daily routine and the standards I set for myself each day to reach my goals. Does every day go as planned? Absolutely not! But if you want to reach your goals and start a successful business, you need to be proactive and make yourself a to-do list for every day each week. Here is a glimpse of my daily routine in hopes that it may help you a bit.

I wake up and I get the kids ready for school. I make my coffee because to me, it's the most important drink of my day. I need that little joy of making my coffee and frothing my oat milk to get my day started in the right direction. Remember, sometimes it is the small things in life that help you stay positive and keep going during your day, so look to the little things that bring you joy.

As the kids are getting ready, I have a "quick to-do check list" that I do daily. I check my messages, emails, and clear out the junk emails, noting which ones are important so I can add them to my schedule for the day. Then I get my social media posting done for my businesses. Some people say that opening your phone first thing in the morning is not a good idea, but for me, it's added stress if I don't get those messages off my list right away in the morning.

As I get ready, I listen to an uplifting and motivating Audible book, podcast, or YouTube video to keep my morning in the proper frame of mind. When I am in the car taking the kids to school, I'm always listening to something upbeat, and sometimes it's what I need to keep me going and my mindset in the right place. I also like to jam out when I'm alone. For me, music speaks to my soul, so it is super important to have when I need it.

Time management is the key to my success. When I get home and start to work, I reheat the coffee and go straight to my desk. I don't let myself get tempted by the TV because I have a certain amount of time in the day to get things done before mom mode kicks in again. Once you master that, you can easily handle unknowns through your day. I have a lot of balls rolling at one time, so I have learned to pivot at points of my day. Believe me, not every day goes as planned—especially with six kids—but as long as the most important tasks in my schedule get done that day, it's a WIN that should be celebrated.

Too many people do not celebrate small wins. It's like they are waiting for a big win that can take so much longer to achieve. Then they get down on themselves, which decreases their spirits. I say, celebrate each day! Have an extra cup of coffee from a coffee shop or have that glass of wine and treat yourself to a non-work-related break. Go ahead and call an encouraging friend and tell them about your small win for the day and then hear theirs so you both can celebrate together. This is key to living your daily life with joy in your heart and a smile on your face.

There are people who will live their lives stuck in a rut without passion. They will hate going to their jobs every morning and they'll be miserable all day dealing with negativity. Then they'll come home and be miserable there, too. It's up to these people to change their life and find their missing puzzle piece. There are choices to be made in this life. You get to decide, choose, and understand which direction you want to go in. It is ultimately your decision. How you make that decision and then shape it into what you need makes all the difference. Find a circle of people and individuals that support you and are emulating exactly the direction you want to go. It's super-duper important in your life's journey towards success and happiness. When you are excited about what you are doing, it is easier to stay on task and get your work done. You wake up with joy in your heart and a smile on your face every morning because you love life, you love what you do, and you love how it helps other people, too.

There are people that are stuck and don't want to stop being stuck, which is basically misery. To me, some of it's their fault and some of it's not. If you're getting to this point of the book and you're like, *Whatever. I've drunk your Kool-Aid up until now and I'm good with my complacent life, thank you. The end,* that's fine. You can stop reading now, because this next part is probably not going to be for you. But for those of you that want more, read on, because it's time to glow up and get yourself to where you want to be.

Time to Glow Up!

Brainstorm your passion. What are your hobbies? Get your creative juices flowing. Make a list of people you know that are passionate about the same things as you and think of ways to reach out to them for advice. Then give them a call or shoot them a text. Let's get the ball rolling!

> **STICKY NOTE MOMENT**
> I am the creator of my passions.

Chapter 10

It's Time to Glow Up

What does it take to embody the person that you want to become? What direction do you need to take? If you want to seriously make changes in your life and become more—a better wife, a better mother, a better business owner, better employee, or better overall person. If you want to help more people, learn how to give grace, how to be kind, how to not judge other people, and how to genuinely help other people in this world, this chapter is all for you!

Fulfilling your heart's passion is a process of rebuilding. It will not come overnight, but nothing good in life is built overnight. You need to make the commitment to yourself to change a few daily tasks and integrate some new habits into your life. It might not come easily at first, but keep those sticky notes in front of you everywhere you go. Put them in your car, at your desk, on your bathroom mirror, and by your nightstand to remind yourself to keep moving forward. You will see them every day and continue to make positive strides in the direction on your path to greatness.

Some things might get in your way and stop you from the thinking positively. It's important to remember that you choose how you react to those fears and unknowns around you. You get to write your own story. You get to drive the car of your own passions. You get to be the one who stands up for what you want and do what it takes for your family to achieve it! You hold the cards in your hand. Nothing will be easy, but knowing you get to choose should make the process of rebuilding that much easier.

Assess yourself with the Comprehensive Glow-Up exercise below. The Glow Up will allow you to glow daily in your life so you can start waking up with joy in your heart. Walking out your door each day with a smile on your face and your head held high! Feeling confident again with who you are and knowing you are amazing! That you are awesome! That you were created for greatness! And that you have a gift to offer this world. Everyone you come in contact with should know that you are a woman on a mission to being the best you can be and creating the life you have always dreamed about. You got this! I believe in you! Link arms with me and all your friends and let's Glow Up together!

The Comprehensive Glow-Up:

1. Grab a pen and paper for writing down your thoughts as you go through this exercise. Assess who you are and your ideal self. Identify areas to work on. Seasons of life change and rebuilding is a part of the seasons and it's a good thing.
2. What are a few undesirable traits you have? Discover the ideal traits you want to cultivate. What

do they mean to you? Remember, this is *your* life, and you are the one who gets to design it!

3. Create a vision board of who you want to be. What do you want your life to look like? What are some goals you have? Include them here. Grab some inspiring pictures and hang them in a place where you will see it each day.

4. Put up encouraging notes to yourself. "I am" statements are key to keeping your mindset positive day in and day out. These are the sticky notes I want you to place everywhere around you. In your car, by your nightstand, on your bathroom mirror, by your chair in the living room, near the stove where you cook every day—everywhere you go daily, put up a sticky note with "I am" statements like: I am amazing. I am beautiful. I am determined. I am powerful. I am a terrific wife. I am the best mom. I am a woman of power. I am passionate. I am peaceful. I am patient. I am kind. I am loyal. I am amazingly organized. Find a few "I am" statements that you want to grow in and write them on your sticky notes. The most important part is to say them out loud, especially in the mirror. This might feel awkward at first, but as you continue to say these "I am" statements to yourself, they will sink into your soul. Slowly but surely, you will start to live out all those beautiful statements that are truly you!

5. Unveil limiting beliefs from your past. To become that ideal person you want to be, we need to dig

deep into your limiting beliefs. What are they? List some that come to mind first. Why do you have them? Who placed them in your mind? How do you let go of them? To let go of these beliefs, you first have to acknowledge that they are not true. The way you talk to yourself is key to mastering your mindset. You must look yourself in the mirror and tell yourself that the limiting beliefs stored in your mind have no purpose or place there. You need to forgive yourself for these beliefs and let go of them once and for all. If you find you cannot, they may be masking anger or blame. Identify these and work on them first. Practice releasing the negative thoughts about yourself and find uplifting people to help you believe in your own self. Those uplifting people will believe in you, so ride on their beliefs until you gain your own.

6. Stop comparing yourself to others. One of the hardest things for women is seeing everyone with their perfect lives and their perfect homes, cars, jobs on social media. It's easy to think that everyone has their stuff together. But in reality, that is not the case. Everyone just shares the good parts of life on social media. But they also have issues and hardships. They are human, too, and they struggle. Most people will not show these parts because being vulnerable is hard. But when you become vulnerable, you open a part of yourself that acknowledges those limiting beliefs. After

Chapter 10: It's Time to Glow Up

you share those parts with others, those people will start to open up and say, "Me too!" It's a beautiful thing to let someone in your life by taking down those walls and sharing your story. That starts a cycle of healing and in the process, others will come to healing, too. The biggest successes in this world are people that share their stories for others to hear. I challenge you to share your story with someone that will take the time to listen and see how you can help each other. I promise you: The more you do this, the more you will feel that confidence start shining.

7. Think of the three most important roles in life that you fill. Write them down. How do you rate yourself from 1 to 10 (1 being terrible and 10 being fantastic in each of those roles)? I would rate myself: Wife: 8; Mom: 8; and Business Owner: 8. As you can see, I still need work in my most important roles, too. We are always going to be a work in progress. Show yourself some self-love and appreciate yourself in the roles you chose. You have done a lot in your life so far and you should be proud of all you have done. So do not be hard on yourself. We are constantly growing and learning, so even if you rate yourself lower in one role, it's okay. We can always work on it. The first step is to acknowledge your rating in each of them. Now, let's get to work on how we can improve.

8. Don't get caught up in what others think of what you are doing in your life. If you are working

towards your dreams for your family, their negativity should not matter. Their criticism is their own, and we can learn and grow from it. This can be hard. Believe me, I struggle with this one the most. As you read this, do you recognize anything you need to make changes on, whether in your life or in your thinking? Are you on the right path? As you go on your path, remember those who cheer you on and the ones who don't. Hold fast to the encouragement from the people who do. And for the people who don't, leave their opinions in the dust. Don't even give them the time of day. They aren't worth it. Their opinions do not pay your bills! You just have to remain strong and know that their opinions mean nothing to the decisions you have made. You are the one in charge of your life and you get to decide!

9. Self-evaluate. Do you do any particular things for self-care? What are those things? If not, why not? Evaluating your self-care can come in all shapes and sizes. Some of these I'm going to list might not seem to you as self-care, but I challenge you to look deeper in these methods. I have learned from my own self-evaluation that a few of these go deeper and help you to relax, rejuvenate, and reset much easier. Yoga, hiking, and walking are excellent, but other methods can help too. Crying, breathing, giving yourself a time-out, and taking a break to laugh are activities that are deeply rejuvenating to

Chapter 10: It's Time to Glow Up

the soul and help you live in the present. I find myself doing these daily and acknowledging their effects so I am aware of how they help me pick up where I left off with my day in the right direction again. A few other great self-care methods are journaling, creating a hobby, and developing a support system. You can also reward yourself with things you love such as a massage, getting your hair done, going for a good coffee, buying a good bottle of wine, going to a concert, or out to dinner. These are all great ways to reward yourself for accomplishing your goals while restoring your strength to keep going on your perfect path.

10. Develop mental toughness. What does that mean to you? For me, it means becoming empowered to be more, to do more, to give everything my all and to know I am created for greatness! You, too, can develop mental toughness to start feeling empowered on your journey to greatness. Being empowered means accepting yourself and taking responsibility for your life! Can you accept yourself? Can you take responsibility? If so, then speak it out loud. Start feeling yourself become empowered! The feeling of doing this exercise will resonate in you. You want to be in the world with a smile on your face, knowing you were created for more and that no one can stand in your way to get there!

11. Discipline yourself. Self-discipline relates to mental toughness, your quality of life, and your

prospective on your life, work, money, and relationships. I heard it once said, "Creating this life will require you to go more in depth on these areas currently in your life." As you grow in your confidence, you will see that self-discipline is key in these areas. When you integrate habits of self-discipline in your daily routine, you will see your confidence rise to new levels. How do you view your life, work, money, and relationships? What area should you work on first as you cultivate your self-discipline? You will become empowered as you take charge of your life in the areas you are looking to grow in.

12. Make a letter of commitment to yourself! Remind yourself of who you want to be and what direction you are going. It is important to share this letter with others so they can hold you accountable on your journey to greatness! Your letter can also inspire others so they, too, can rebuild their confidence in self-esteem and finances! The more we share where we want to be, the more we speak that into the world, and the more you will see God's work around you! You got this, girlie! Together, we will rebuild our confidence and find our gifts on our journey to finding our greatness!

So, what's it going to be, momma? Are you willing to master your momma mindset to rebuild your confidence? To find your gift? To fulfill your greatness? The choice is yours. The gift you have to offer this world is

Chapter 10: It's Time to Glow Up

inside of you, and you deserve to find it and use it to fulfill your dreams and goals. I'm here waiting to link arms with you and cheer you on! Are you ready to wake up each day with a smile on your face and joy in your heart? I believe in you... Do *you* believe in you? Let's Glow together, Girl!

Chapter 11

I Am

Remember:

I will embrace the unknowns and find a positive from every fear that comes my way.

I can and I will find the good in every problem.

I am amazing at releasing control.

I will step out of my comfort zone to walk through my doors of opportunity.

I am in charge of my emotions.

I am able to stop, listen, and just... be.

I can walk through sorrow to find joy.

I am the creator of my passions.

About the Author

Krissy lives in a small town in Pennsylvania in what she calls her perfect mountain dream house. When she is not busy wrangling six children, she strives to encourage and inspire women to live their best lives and rebuild their confidence inside and out.

If you would like to connect with Krissy, be sure to check out the websites below.

https://inphone.co/krissycressler

www.krissycressler.com

https://krissycressler.podia.com

Made in the USA
Columbia, SC
11 October 2022